W0038377

NEW VANGUARD 339

GERMAN TANKS IN
BARBAROSSA 1941

STEVEN J. ZALOGA   ILLUSTRATED BY FELIPE RODRÍGUEZ

OSPREY PUBLISHING

Bloomsbury Publishing Plc

Kemp House, Chawley Park, Cumnor Hill, Oxford OX2 9PH, UK

Bloomsbury Publishing Ireland Limited,

29 Earlsfort Terrace, Dublin 2, D02 AY28, Ireland

1385 Broadway, 5th Floor, New York, NY 10018, USA

E-mail: info@ospreypublishing.com

www.ospreypublishing.com

OSPREY is a trademark of Osprey Publishing Ltd

First published in Great Britain in 2025

© Osprey Publishing Ltd, 2025

All rights reserved. No part of this publication may be: i) reproduced or transmitted in any form, electronic or mechanical, including photocopying, recording or by means of any information storage or retrieval system without prior permission in writing from the publishers; or ii) used or reproduced in any way for the training, development or operation of artificial intelligence (AI) technologies, including generative AI technologies. The rights holders expressly reserve this publication from the text and data mining exception as per Article 4(3) of the Digital Single Market Directive (EU) 2019/790.

A catalog record for this book is available from the British Library.

ISBN: PB 9781472864406; eBook 9781472864376; ePDF 9781472864383; XML: 9781472864390

25 26 27 28 29   10 9 8 7 6 5 4 3 2 1

Index by Mark Swift

Typeset by PDQ Digital Media Solutions, Bungay, UK

Printed by Repro India Ltd.

Osprey Publishing supports the Woodland Trust, the UK's leading woodland conservation charity.

To find out more about our authors and books visit www.ospreypublishing.com. Here you will find extracts, author interviews, details of forthcoming events and the option to sign up for our newsletter.

For product safety related questions contact productsafety@bloomsbury.com

Title page image: see p. 17.

AUTHOR'S NOTE

Unless otherwise specified, the photos in this book are from the author's collection.

CONTENTS

GERMAN TANKS IN *BARBAROSSA* 1941

INTRODUCTION

Operation *Barbarossa* involved the largest tank confrontations in history until the final campaigns of 1945. Although the Kursk campaign in 1943 is often cited as the war's largest tank engagement, *Barbarossa* involved over 4,000 German tanks and assault guns against 20,000 Soviet tanks; four times more tanks than Kursk. Likewise, individual battles of the campaign, such as Brody-Dubno in June 1941, involved five times as many tanks as the largest 1943 battle of the Kursk campaign at Prokhorovka, which has been widely mistaken as the world's largest tank battle.

The Panzer force was the most critical element of the German *Barbarossa* plan. The speed and shock value of the Panzer divisions was essential for the Wehrmacht to prevail over the Red Army in a brief campaign of annihilation. *Barbarossa* failed, and problems with the Panzers were a significant reason for this defeat.

Traditional accounts of the Soviet–German conflict in 1941 have contended that the defeat of the Wehrmacht at the gates of Moscow in December 1941 was the key to the failure of *Barbarossa*. More recent scholarship, such the David Stahel's trilogy, have argued that the Wehrmacht attack lost momentum in the late summer and early autumn, ensuring the failure of *Barbarossa* far earlier than the arrival of the Russian winter.

This book examines this issue from the standpoint of the Panzer force. Such a short volume cannot possibly cover all the major battles or the larger strategic issues. These are already covered in other Osprey books. Instead, this book focuses on the issue of whether the Panzer force had the resiliency to conduct a high-tempo campaign for more than a few months. The evidence presented here suggests that durability of the Panzers was not sufficient to maintain combat effectiveness beyond the summer. By early autumn, the Panzer divisions fell to less than half-strength and the Panzer attacks lost their critical momentum.

DOCTRINE AND ORGANIZATION

For the German High Command of the Army (*OKH: Oberkommando des Heeres*), the spearhead of Operation *Barbarossa* was the *Panzerkeil* (Panzer wedge). This term is usually understood as a description for a type

A column from Pz.Rgt.15, 11.Panzer-Division led by a PzKpfw III Ausf. H while taking part in Operation *25*, the invasion of Yugoslavia in April 1941 prior to the start of Operation *Barbarossa*.

of small-unit tactical formation. But in the vocabulary of the senior German military commanders in 1941, it referred to the *Schnelltruppen* (fast troops) of the Wehrmacht. The two basic maneuver formations were the Panzer division and the motorized infantry division. The latter is better known by its subsequent designation as a Panzergrenadier division.

The Panzerkeil was the most decisive element of the plan for Operation *Barbarossa*, since the rapid envelopment and destruction of the Red Army were the main operational goals. As was the case in France, the Panzer divisions and motorized infantry divisions were used in a highly concentrated fashion.

Each Army Group (*HG: Heeresgruppe*) received at least one Panzergruppe as its principal maneuver element. Since *Heeresgruppe Mitte* (center) was the *Schwerpunkt* (focal point) of the assault, it received two Panzergruppen. Each Panzergruppe was based around two or three corps. These corps were officially designated as Armee Korps (Motorisiert) in 1941, though usually referred to as Panzer Korps, a practice followed in this book. A total of 17 Panzer divisions were committed to the opening phase of Operation *Barbarossa*.

A tank column from Pz.Rgt.15, 11.Panzer-Division enters a Ukrainian village during the summer 1941 campaign with a PzKpfw III Ausf. J nearest the camera. The "K" marking on the tanks was for Werner Kempf, commander of XLVIII.Panzer Korps to which the division was attached.

Following the 1940 campaigns in western Europe, the Wehrmacht was committed to two related campaigns in the Balkans in April 1941 against Greece and Yugoslavia prior to Operation *Barbarossa*. The Balkan campaign involved the use of seven Panzer divisions. Controversies linger about whether these operations delayed *Barbarossa* and undermined its prospects. All these Panzer divisions were subsequently committed to *Barbarossa* except for two. The 2.Panzer-Division lost a considerable amount of equipment in May 1941 when two of its transport ships from Greece

were sunk. It was rebuilt in Germany and subsequently served as a theater reserve in the Lwów/Przemyśl area of southeastern Poland at the start of the campaign. After the Balkans campaign, the 5.Panzer-Division was sent back to the Berlin area for refitting with tropical equipment for potential commitment to North Africa. In the event, both the 2.Panzer-Division and 5.Panzer-Division were committed to *Barbarossa* in September 1941 as reinforcements prior to the start of Operation *Taifun*, bringing the total number of Panzer divisions on the *Ostfront* (Eastern Front) to 19.

German tactical doctrine for Operation *Barbarossa* was essentially similar to the French campaign. The Panzerkeil was expected to conduct the initial breakthrough of the Soviet defenses as well as the subsequent breakout into the Soviet rear areas. Their operational goal was to surround and disrupt the forward-deployed Soviet forces in the initial phase of the campaign. The Panzerkeil was followed by the remainder of the German infantry divisions. Since they were dependent on horse-transport, they were significantly slower than the Panzer and motorized divisions. This infantry wave was assigned to defeat surrounded Soviet forces and to mop up behind the Panzerkeil.

Operation *Barbarossa* Panzer organization			
HG Nord	**Generalfeldmarschall Wilhelm Ritter von Leeb**		
Panzergruppe.4	**GenOberst Erich Hoepner**		
XLI.Panzer Korps	Gen d.Pz.Tr. Georg-Hans Reinhardt	1.Pz.Div.	6.Pz.Div.
LVI.Panzer Korps	Gen d.Inf. Erich von Manstein	8.Pz.Div.	
HG Mitte	**Generalfeldmarschall Fedor von Bock**		
Panzergruppe.3	**GenOberst Hermann Hoth**		
XXXIX.Panzer Korps	Gen d.Pz.Tr. Rudolf Schmidt	7.Pz.Div.	20.Pz.Div
LVII.Panzer Korps	Gen d.Pz.Tr. Adolf Kuntzen	12.Pz.Div.	19.Pz.Div.
Panzergruppe.2	**GenOberst Heinz Guderian**		
XXIV.Panzer Korps	Gen d.Pz.Tr. Leo Geyr von Schweppenburg	3.Pz.Div.	4.Pz.Div.
XLVI.Panzer Korps	GenOberst Heinrich von Vietinghoff-Scheel	10.Pz.Div.	
XLVII.Panzer Korps	Gen d.Art. Joachim Lemelsen	17.Pz.Div.	18.Pz.Div.
HG Süd	**Generalfeldmarschall Gerd von Rundstedt**		
Panzergruppe.1	**Generalfeldmarschall Ewald von Kleist**		
III.Panzer Korps	GenOberst Eberhard von Mackensen	13.Pz.Div.	14.Pz.Div.
XIV.Panzer Korps	Gen d.Inf. Gustav von Wietersheim	9.Pz.Div.	16.Pz.Div
XLVIII.Panzer Korps	Gen d.Pz.Tr. Werner Kempf	11.Pz.Div.	

There were notable changes in the composition of the Panzer divisions between the Battle of France in 1940 and Operation *Barbarossa* in June 1941. The composition of the Panzer divisions became more uniform, the equipment improved, and there was an increase in the other combat arms.

The early Panzer divisions were tank-heavy and infantry-light, having as many as two Panzer regiments but only a single motorized infantry (*Schützen*) regiment. Some 1940 Panzer divisions had in the vicinity of 300 tanks, with the 4.Panzer-Division being the largest with 366 tanks. However, four of the Panzer divisions had only a single Panzer regiment. So, divisional strength in 1940 varied considerably from a low of 156 to a high of 366. On average, a 1940 division had 265 tanks.

The Wehrmacht decided to double the number of Panzer divisions in 1941 from ten to 20 to deal with the geographical vastness of the Soviet Union. This was accomplished by limiting each division to a single Panzer regiment.

As a result, the average strength of the Panzer divisions fell from 265 in 1940 to 175 in 1941. Even though the average Panzer division had fewer tanks than in 1940, the overall combat effectiveness of Panzer regiments increased due to a substantial improvement in the types of tanks in use. In 1940, more than half (55.6 percent) of the Panzers were the less effective light tanks such as the Panzerkampfwagen (PzKpfw) I and PzKpfw II. In 1941, the percentage of these obsolete tanks fell to about a quarter of the force, 23.9 percent. One of the most important changes in Panzer strength was the advent of the PzKpfw III with the new 5cm tank gun. None of these were available in the 1940 campaign, while in 1941 they amounted to about a fifth (20.2 percent) of the force.

A PzKpfw III Ausf. H of 3./Pz.Abt. z.b.V.40 near Vuokkiniemi in Russian Karelia on July 11 with a Finnish army guide on the engine deck during the efforts to cut the Murmansk road. (SA-kuva)

The Panzer regiment was based on three Panzer battalions (*Abteilungen*) each of which had two light and one medium tank companies. The light tank companies were based around the PzKpfw III, though shortages of this type meant that Czechoslovak light tanks were used in its place in six of the 20 existing divisions. The medium company was based on the PzKpfw IV, nominally with four tanks per platoon (*Zug*) though in practice with three per platoon due to lingering shortages of this type. The PzKpfw II was deployed on a scale of one platoon in each light and medium tank company. An essential element of Panzer formations was the *Befehlspanzer*, a command tank equipped with additional radios.

The infantry element in the Panzer division doubled between 1940 and 1941. Instead of a single Schützen regiment in most 1940 Panzer divisions, the 1941 divisions had two Schützen regiments. The number of armored half-tracks (*mSPW: mittlere Schützenpanzerwagen*) also substantially increased. At the time of the Battle of France, there were less than a dozen Schützen companies equipped with the Sd.Kfz.251 armored half-track, mostly concentrated in the 1.Panzer-Division that had seven companies. By June 1941, about 575 Sd.Kfz.251 were in service with the Panzer divisions. The objective was about 150 per division, so only about a fifth of the table of equipment had been realized at the start of the campaign. The half-tracks were most heavily concentrated in the 1. and 10.Panzer-Divisionen. The remaining divisions had about 20–27 half-tracks each. The exceptions were three divisions (14., 16., 19.) that had only a handful. The relatively modest number of armored half-tracks available in 1941 did not permit full mechanization of the division's infantry, but it marked an important step in the development of combined-arms tactics compared to the rudimentary tactics of 1940.

Other important improvements were made to the 1941 Panzer divisions. A heavy 15cm howitzer battalion was added, and the Panzergrenadiers received far more light and heavy infantry guns for direct support.

Another difference between the 1940 and 1941 campaigns was the growth of non-divisional armored units, categorized as *Heerestruppen* (army troops) since they were attached to high commands for support. Five separate Panzer *Abteilungen* (battalions) were deployed for Operation *Barbarossa*. Three of

This PzKpfw B2 (F), tactical number 224, used the second configuration of this flamethrower tank with the Köbe type of flamethrower. Pz.Abt.(F).102 supported the 296.Infanterie-Division on June 26–28, 1941 during the attack against the Wielki Dział strongpoint, part of the Red Army's 6th Rawsko-Ruski Fortified Zone of the Molotov line on the old Soviet–Polish border. This unit was dissolved on July 27 after barely a month in combat due to the decrepit state of its equipment.

these were flamethrower battalions (Pz.Abt.(F): Panzer-Abteilung Flamm). Two of these were equipped with the PzKpfw II (F) Flamingo and one with the PzKpfw B2 (F). These were intended to deal with the border fortifications of the Molotov and Stalin lines. The Pz.Abt.(F).100 was attached to the 18.Panzer-Division, the Pz.Abt.(F).101 to the 7.Panzer-Division, and the Pz.Abt.(F).102 to the 24.Infanterie-Division. There were also two separate tank battalions deployed to Finland, Pz.Abt.211 using war-booty French tanks, and Pz.Abt. z.b.V.40 with a mixed assortment of tanks.

The most significant difference between 1940 and 1941 was the considerable expansion of the assault gun (*StuG: Sturmgeschütz*) force. These vehicles were raised and trained by the artillery branch and were used for direct infantry support. During the Battle of France, there were only four batteries in service. By the time of Operation *Barbarossa*, this had increased nearly ten-fold to 11 StuG Abteilungen and five separate StuG Batterien with a total of 339 StuG committed to Operation *Barbarossa*.

The *Heeres Waffenamt* (HWA: Army weapons department) began developing dedicated tank destroyers in 1940 using obsolete light tank chassis armed with Czech 4.7cm anti-tank guns. These were used to form *Panzerjäger Abteilungen* (tank destroyer battalions). A total of 233 tank destroyers were deployed for Operation *Barbarossa* in nine battalions and a few separate companies.

 A

PzKpfw III DURING OPERATION *BARBAROSSA*

1. PzKpfw III Ausf. J, Stabskompanie, II./Pz.Rgt.18, 18.Panzer-Division, Panzergruppe.2.
The standard camouflage scheme on Wehrmacht tanks in 1941 was an overall finish of Dunkelgrau Nr. 46 (dark gray), later redesignated as RAL 7021. Divisional markings as shown here were usually in chrome yellow while tactical markings such as turret numbers were in white or yellow. The tanks of the headquarters company as seen here usually had a tactical number starting in Roman numerals as I (Abteilung I.) or II (Abteilung II.) followed by numbers indicating battalion commander, executive officer, etc. In this case, the order is reversed with the tank number followed by the battalion number in Roman numerals.

2. PzKpfw III Ausf J, 6./II./Pz.Rgt.3, 2.Panzer-Division. Pz.Rgt.3 had a tradition of using intricate markings on each company's tanks. For example, in 1939–40, 1.Kompanie used playing card symbols. During 1941, 6.Kompanie used geometric symbols surmounted with a winged dragon with each company identified by a color. This color was also carried over to the usual Panzer Kompanie rhomboid symbol. The precise color pattern has not been recorded but is believed to have been green (*Stab Zug*), blue (*1.Zug*), red (*2.Zug*) and yellow (*3.Zug*). The divisional insignia was painted in the usual chrome yellow.

Unit	Pz.I*	Pz.II	Pz.35(t)**	Pz.38(t)**	Pz.III***	Pz.IV	Bef.Pz.III	Beute	Total
1.Pz.Div.	11	43			0+71	20	11		156
3.Pz.Div.	13	58			29+81	32	15		228
4.Pz.Div.	10	44			31+74	20	8		187
6.Pz.Div.	11	47	160			30	8		256
7.Pz.Div.	11	53		174		30	8		276
8.Pz.Div.	11	49		125		30	8		223
9.Pz.Div.	19	32			11+60	20	12		154
10.Pz.Div.	11	45			0+105	20	12		193
11.Pz.Div.	11	44			24+47	20	8		154
12.Pz.Div.	51	33		117		30			231
13.Pz.Div.	8	45			27+44	20	13		157
14.Pz.Div.	11	45			15+56	20	11		158
16.Pz.Div.	12	45			23+48	20	10		158
17.Pz.Div.	22	44			0+106	30	10		212
18.Pz.Div.	72	50			99+15	36	12		284
19.Pz.Div.	53	35		121		30			239
20.Pz.Div.	55	31		123		31			240
H.Tr.Pz.Abt.	48	143			25		10	73	299
Total	*144+296*	*886*	*149+11*	*625+35*	*284+707*	*439*	*156*	*73*	*3,805*

*Panzer + kleiner Befehlspanzer and PzKpfw I mit Abwurfvorrichtung

**Panzer + Befehlspanzer

***3.7cm + 5cm

The accompanying chart shows the strength of the Panzer divisions as well as Heerestruppen Panzer Abteilungen. Besides these separate tank battalions, the other types of armored formations contained a further 339 StuG assault guns and 233 Panzerjäger tank destroyers for a grand total of 4,377 tanks and AFVs at the start of Operation *Barbarossa*.

TANKS OF GERMANY'S ALLIES

Germany's five allied armies contributed a further 549 tanks to Operation *Barbarossa*, though 121 of these were decrepit tankettes. A sixth ally, Bulgaria, permitted German troop passage through its territory but did not take an active role in combat.

Romania

Romania was Germany's largest ally at the start of Operation *Barbarossa*, with two Romanian field armies serving with Heeresgruppe Süd in Ukraine. Prior to the 1941 campaign, the Romanian army had raised two tank regiments. The 1st Tank Regiment (*Regimentul 1 Care de Luptă*) was equipped with the R-2 light tank, a version of the LT vz 35/PzKpfw 35(t), while the 2nd Tank Regiment was equipped with the French R35 light tank. Romania was unable to expand this force after the German high command refused Romanian requests for the purchase of more modern tanks from the occupied Czech tank plants. On paper, the Romanian tank units were consolidated into a new Armored Division (*Divizei Blindate*) in 1941 but, in practice, the new division did not fight as a unified formation in the summer 1941 campaign.

A Romanian R-2c light tank of the *Regimentul 1 Care de Luptă*, 3rd Romanian Army in Ukraine in 1941. These Škoda LT vz 35 tanks were purchased from Czechoslovakia before the war.

The 1st Tank Regiment was divided up, with one battalion of R-2s supporting the 3rd Romanian Army and the other the 4th Romanian Army. The R-2 tanks saw considerable fighting during the summer campaign which concluded with the bloody siege of the port of Odessa on the Black Sea. Romanian tank losses were substantial, though more often from mechanical exhaustion than combat. At the end of August 1941, barely 20 of the regiment's original 105 R-2 tanks were operational. During the 1941 campaign, the 1st Tank Regiment suffered 26 combat losses of its R-2 tanks and 60 were broken down. In early 1942, 40 R-2s were sent back to Škoda in Plzeň (Pilsen) for overhaul and a further 50 tanks were sent back to the Škoda automobile repair shop in Ploieşti, Romania, for less-extensive repairs. As a result, the 1st Tank Regiment was nearly devoid of tanks through early 1942. To make up for Romanian losses, in October 1941 Berlin finally consented to sell the Romanians their surviving inventory 26 PzKpfw 35(t). These tanks were overhauled by Škoda and delivered in June–July 1942 in time for the disastrous Stalingrad campaign.

A Hungarian Toldi light tank of the Fast Corps (*Gyorshadtest*) in combat in Ukraine in the summer of 1941.

Hungary

Hungary supported the German invasion of Yugoslavia in the spring of 1941, using a Fast Corps (*Gyorshadtest*) that included three mechanized brigades. The Hungarian contingent in *Barbarossa* served with Heeresgruppe Süd and initially involved the same three brigades of the Fast Corps as used in Yugoslavia. This totaled 60 Ansaldo L3 tankettes and 81 Toldi light tanks. The Toldi was a version of the Swedish L-60 light tank that was license-produced in Hungary. It was roughly

A pair of Škoda LT vz 35 of the Slovak Fast Corps under repair in Ukraine on July 13, 1941.

comparable to the German PzKpfw II. The short Yugoslav campaign led to the mechanical enfeeblement of many of the participating Hungarian tanks and tankettes.

The Hungarian Fast Corps fought from Nikolayev in Ukraine to Izium on the Donets River, a distance of some 1,000km. The corps was withdrawn back to Hungary on November 15, 1941 after all of its Ansaldo tankettes and 80 percent of its Toldi light tanks had become unserviceable, primarily due to mechanical exhaustion rather than combat losses.

Slovakia

When Germany completed the absorption of the Czech provinces into the Reich in 1939, it permitted Slovakia to remain independent as a fascist ally. The Slovak army had 79 Škoda LT vz 35 tanks on hand in 1939, a type better known as the PzKpfw 35(t) when in Wehrmacht use. When Slovakia agreed to join Operation *Barbarossa*, Germany permitted the transfer of additional tanks manufactured in the occupied Czech territories including 32 PzKpfw 38(t) Ausf. S and 21 LT vz 40 light tanks. These were used to form a tank battalion (Kobornia) in the Slovak Mobile Group that took part in the invasion as part of Heeresgruppe Süd.

Italy

For Operation *Barbarossa*, Italy deployed 8a Armata (8th Army) also known as the ARMIR (*Armata Italiana in Russia)*. Due to its heavy commitments in North Africa, the armored component of the ARMIR was tiny. Its only significant armored force was the *III Gruppo Corazzato "San Giorgio"* (3rd San Giorgio Armored Group) of the CSIR Fast Corps (*Corpo di spedizione italiano in Russia*) which included 61 L3 tankettes. These tankettes saw combat starting on August 10 during the fighting between the Dniester and Bug rivers in Ukraine. The group supported the Pasubio Division in late September and November 1941. By Christmas, the group had lost most of its tankettes in combat or due to mechanical exhaustion.

CV35 tankettes of *III Gruppo Corazzato "San Giorgio"* pass a column of Italian trucks in Ukraine during the summer 1941 campaign.

Finland

Finland agreed to join Operation *Barbarossa* in the hopes of recovering the Karelian lands taken by the Soviet Union in the 1939–40 war. Finland captured large numbers of Soviet tanks in the 1939–40 fighting and these were used to form new armored units raised in 1940–41. The Finnish Tank Battalion (*PsvP: Panssarivaunupataljoona*) had been equipped with Vickers 6-ton tanks

and Renault FT light tanks. It was enlarged and modernized so that in 1941 it had three tank companies, a heavy tank platoon and three armored car platoons. The Vickers 6-ton tanks were improved by re-arming them with captured Soviet 45mm tank guns, sometimes called T-26E. At the start of Operation *Barbarossa*, the Finnish Army had 29 T-37 amphibious tanks, 13 T-38 amphibious tanks, 26 Vickers light tanks, ten T-26 Model 1931, 20 T-26 Model 1933, four T-26 Model 1937, two T-28 medium tanks, two OT-26 flamethrower tanks, four OT-130 flamethrower tanks, and a small number of older, obsolete types. Finland also acquired six Landsverk Anti 40mm self-propelled guns from Sweden. After regaining the lost Finnish territories in the summer and fall of 1941, the Finnish Army restricted its further combat actions despite German pressure to assist in the capture of Leningrad and the port of Archangel. The Finnish Army suffered few tank casualties in the 1941 campaign and managed to capture additional Soviet tanks including a few modern types such as the T-34 and KV.

Finnish tank crews at their base at Äänislinna. The tanks in the foreground are Vickers 6-ton tanks upgraded with captured Soviet 45mm tank guns. They were sometimes called T-26E as a result. (SA-kuva)

TECHNICAL FACTORS

The Panzers used in combat in the summer of 1941 were similar to those in the Battle of France in 1940.[1] There were two principal differences. It was obvious that the 3.7cm gun was no longer effective for fighting the better enemy tanks, so a new 5cm gun began to appear on the PzKpfw III. The Wehrmacht did not anticipate the appearance of newer Soviet types such as the T-34 and KV, and so the 5cm gun immediately proved to be inadequate. The Soviet tank threat would necessitate a steady increase in tank firepower in 1942, including a longer 5cm gun, as well as the introduction of long-barreled 7.5cm guns on the PzKpfw IV and StuG III.

The other major change was an increase in tank frontal armor due to encounters with the French 25mm and 47mm gun, and the British 2-pdr in 1940. The larger types such as the PzKpfw III and PzKpfw IV had their frontal hull armor increased to 60mm, initially by adding appliqué armor, and subsequently increasing the thickness of the basic armor. Lighter tanks had lesser amounts of added armor. This provided good frontal protection against the

Germany assisted Bulgaria in building up its 1-vi Tank Polk with the sale or transfer of PzKpfw 35(t) and Renault R35 tanks, adding to a small existing force of L3 tankettes and Vickers light tanks. Although allied to Germany, the Bulgarians did not participate in Operation *Barbarossa*.

1   For more details, see: Steven Zaloga, *German Tanks in France 1940*, Osprey New Vanguard 327, 2024.

standard Soviet 45mm tank and anti-tank guns. However, it was inadequate against the newer Soviet 76mm guns.

Aside from these obvious changes, there was a general effort undertaken by the HWA to simplify designs to increase production. The Wehrmacht was still short of tanks, and production increases were a major concern.

The Battle of France in May–June 1940 provided some rough guidelines about tank attrition in combat. German Panzer losses in the first three weeks of fighting in May 1940 were 604 tanks, about 23 percent of the starting strength. By the time that the Wehrmacht had reached Dunkirk, about half of the Panzer force was still operational with tanks in repair and total losses constituting the remainder. The Wehrmacht identified total losses (*Totalausfall*) as Panzers that had suffered irredeemable battle damage or were in enemy hands. Tanks that had been knocked out in combat but could be rebuilt either in field depots or back in Germany were considered in long-term repair. As a result, some of the tanks in the repair category were in fact useless for the remainder of the campaign. Total German Panzer losses in the 1940 battles amounted to 839 tanks, 31 percent of the total starting strength of the Panzer force. A further 1,700 German tanks underwent factory repair and rebuilding through early 1941 to deal with combat damage, mechanical problems, and necessary upgrades.

Wehrmacht tank strength June–December 1941							
Type	Jun	Jul	Aug	Sep	Oct	Nov	Dec
PzKpfw I	877	843	771	642	681	717	728
PzKpfw II	1074	1067	955	900	896	859	881
PzKpfw 35(t)	187	189	189	191	191	191	192
PzKpfw 38(t)	754	763	661	543	547	528	434
PzKpfw III (3.7cm)	350	327	268	243	227	216	203
PzKpfw III (5cm)	1,090	1,174	1,211	1,328	1,419	1,527	1,622
PzKpfw IV	517	537	488	470	499	485	511
PzBefWg	330	331	331	335	328	315	318
Panzer sub-total	*5,179*	*5,231*	*4,874*	*4,652*	*4,788*	*4,838*	*4,889*
StuG III	377	416	461	479	508	566	598
Panzer + AFV total	*5,556*	*5,647*	*5,335*	*5,131*	*5,296*	*5,404*	*5,487*

PzKpfw III

The backbone of the Panzer force in Operation *Barbarossa* was the PzKpfw III. At the time of the Battle of France in 1940, the principal versions in service were the PzKpfw III Ausf. E and Ausf. F. These were essentially the same except for the switch from the Maybach HL 120 TR engine to the HL 120 TRM with improved magnetos on the Ausf. F. The early PzKpfw III had

B **PzKpfw IV DURING OPERATION *BARBAROSSA***

1. PzKpfw IV Ausf. E, 8./II./Pz.Rgt.1, 1.Panzer-Division, Panzergruppe.4, 1941. German tactical numbers followed a standard pattern indicating company/platoon/tank, so in this case, 821 indicated 8.Kompanie, 2.Zug, Panzer.1. The style of tactical numbers varied from regiment to regiment with some preferring a small and simple number as in this case, while others used larger and more prominent numbers as on the accompanying plate.

2. PzKpfw IV Ausf. D, 6./II./Pz.Rgt.27, 19.Panzer-Division, Panzergruppe.3, 1941. Some Panzer regiments used large tactical numbers as seen here with 621 in red with white trim. It also carried the divisional Wolfsangel insignia on the front and side superstructure. This PzKpfw IV Ausf. D has the bolted appliqué armor upgrade.

1

2

Some older PzKpfw III variants were still in service during Operation *Barbarossa* such as this PzKpfw III Ausf. D serving with Pz.Abt. z.b.V.40 in Lapland in northern Finland during the German attempts in the winter of 1941–42 to capture the Soviet ports such as Murmansk on the Kola peninsula. (SA-kuva)

been plagued with problems with its Zahnradfabrik Variorex transmission but these issues had largely been resolved by the end of 1940. The most critical improvement regarding the PzKpfw III was the expansion of its production base from a single Daimler-Benz plant to five other plants to increase production. As a result, the allotment of the PzKpfw III to the Panzer divisions in 1941 was close to the official KStN (*Kriegs Stärke Nachweisungen*: war establishment strength).

The PzKpfw III Ausf. E/F was armed with a 3.7cm gun. In January 1938, the HWA had been authorized to begin work on a better gun. This was prompted by growing recognition that the 3.7cm gun was not adequate to deal with newer British and French tanks with thicker armor. The use of a new 5cm gun had been the source of bureaucratic controversy since 1936, with the 3.7cm gun retained on the PzKpfw III through 1940 to ensure standardization with the infantry's 3.7cm anti-tank gun. The proposed 5cm tank gun would require a new family of ammunition, and some departments in the army were unwilling to support such a costly and disruptive innovation. Resistance was overcome due to the growing recognition of the threat posed by thicker enemy tank armor. Work on both a new 5cm tank gun and a new 5cm towed anti-tank gun for the infantry was initiated in 1938. Production of the PzKpfw III Ausf. G with the 5cm gun was planned to begin in June 1940 but the first tanks were not accepted until July and so were not in service during the Battle of France.

A PzKpfw III Ausf. F with I./Pz.Rgt.33, 9.Panzer-Division on the Ostfront in July 1941. This tank underwent the *Umbewaffnung Programm* that substituted the 5cm gun for the 3.7cm, added frontal armor, and made numerous other improvements.

The new 5cm gun could penetrate 46mm of armor at 30 degrees at 500 meters. This meant that it could not penetrate the frontal armor of the T-34 or KV tank when using the standard Panzergranate 39 projectile. It could penetrate the vast majority of older Soviet types. There was some recognition that the new gun was inadequate against heavier enemy tanks. One means to improve its performance was to use a new generation of high-velocity armor-piercing projectile, the Panzergranate 40. This type of ammunition used a dense tungsten carbide core contained within a mild steel body fitted with a light ballistic cap. This permitted a substantial increase in velocity, from 685m/s in the case of the normal 5cm PzGr.39 projectile to 1,050m/s for the tungsten carbide PzGr.40. At short range (100m), this had a dramatic difference in armor penetration, 55mm for the old ammunition compared to 97mm with the new tungsten carbide projectile, meaning that it could penetrate the frontal armor of the T-34. This advantage dissipated quickly at range,

so that at 500mm the old PzGr.39 could penetrate 46mm while the PzGr.40 could penetrate 58mm, giving it marginal performance frontally against the T-34. Similar tungsten carbide ammunition was also developed for other guns such as the various 37mm guns. The main problem was that tungsten carbide was available in very limited amounts since it was reserved for use for machine tools in the defense industry. As a result, supplies were minuscule with most German tanks receiving only about five rounds of this type in the summer of 1941.

A PzKpfw III Ausf. H of Pz.Abt. z.b.V.40 on July 1, 1941 showing the 30mm appliqué armor bolted to the hull front. (SA-kuva)

Production shifted to the PzKpfw III Ausf. H in October 1940. This introduced a new turret design that incorporated an improved gun mantlet and thickened armor. In addition, frontal armor was increased by adding 30mm plates to the hull front, increasing the armor thickness to 60mm. This was proof against frontal attack by typical enemy guns of the time such as the Soviet 45mm gun. Production of the PzKpfw III Ausf. H was short-lived, ending in April 1941 in favor of the PzKpfw III Ausf. J. This version was essentially similar, but instead of front armor of 30+30mm, it used homogenous 50mm armor. There were numerous small design improvements, such as the new hull machine-gun mount with a ball-shaped cover. By the time of the start of Operation *Barbarossa*, over three-quarters of the PzKpfw III were the newer versions armed with the 5cm gun.

A PzKpfw III Ausf. J of Pz.Rgt.35, 4.Panzer-Division in occupied Poland in May 1941 prior to *Barbarossa*. This tank has been fitted with some of the combing for the *Tauchpanzer* deep wading system.

PzKpfw IV

The PzKpfw IV had been designed to support the PzKpfw III with heavier firepower in the form of a short 7.5cm gun. This weapon was not designed for fighting enemy tanks, but rather was intended for general fire support missions using high-explosive ammunition. It had proven to be an excellent design during the fighting

A PzKpfw IV Ausf. E of Pz.Rgt.35, 4.Panzer-Division with Guderian's Panzergruppe.2 in Belarus on July 9, 1941.

in Poland and France, even though these campaigns revealed the need for heavier armor to resist new enemy anti-tank guns. The PzKpfw IV Ausf. E, manufactured through April 1941, had a basic 30mm superstructure front with 30mm armor appliqués. It was followed by the PzKpfw IV Ausf. F that increased the basic frontal armor to 50mm with a 10mm appliqué. It also used a simplified superstructure front. This was the standard production type through early 1942.

PzKpfw 38(t)

When Germany occupied the Czech provinces in 1939, it inherited the small but sophisticated Czech tank industry. The best of the new Czech tanks, the LT 38, was an essential ingredient in enlarging the Panzer force in the Blitzkrieg years of 1939–41. The German light tanks were armed with machine guns and 20mm cannon, but the Czech tanks offered an excellent 37mm gun, comparable to that on the PzKpfw III medium tank. The Wehrmacht decided to continue LT 38 production to speed up the equipment of the Panzer divisions. The LT 38 was initially designated as the PzKpfw III(t) in German service but later redesignated as the PzKpfw 38(t) to avoid confusion with the PzKpfw III tank. The PzKpfw 38(t) was smaller and lighter than the PzKpfw III, and closer in size to the PzKpfw II. Its most significant

C

PzKpfw 38(T) DURING OPERATION *BARBAROSSA*

1. PzKpfw 38(t) Befehlswagen, Stabs-Kompanie, II.Abteilung, Pz.Rgt.27, 19.Panzer-Division. This is the command tank of the II.Abteilung commander as indicated by the tactical number II01. The Roman "II" in this number is oddly illustrated, missing the lower serifs. The PzKpfw 38(t) was notoriously cramped inside and lacked the space for carrying the crew's equipment. As a result, some units modified their tanks by adding sheet metal stowage bins. This tank has both added side bins as well as a bin on the rear of the turret. This unit also had jerrican stowage added on the fenders behind the side bin.

2. PzKpfw 38(t) Ausf. E/F, 5./Pz.Rgt.27, 19.Panzer-Division. As in the case of the Befehlswagen shown here, this PzKpfw 38(t) Ausf. E/F has the typical side stowage bins added by Pz.Rgt.27 but lacks the rear turret bin more commonly seen on command tanks. The tactical number on this tank is in an untypical font. It indicates 5.Kompanie, 2.Zug, Panzer Nr.2 that was part of the II. Abteilung.

1

2

A column of PzKpfw 38(t) of Pz.Rgt.25, 7.Panzer-Division begins to move into Lithuania on June 22, 1941.

tactical shortcoming was the use of a two-man turret that was inferior to the three-man layout of the PzKpfw III. However, the narrow hull of the PzKpfw 38(t) precluded the development of a larger turret with a three-man crew.

During its production, the PzKpfw 38(t) underwent a string of modifications, some to improve its combat qualities and some to better integrate it into German service. The PzKpfw 38(t) Ausf. C manufactured from May to August 1940 increased the front hull armor from 25mm to 40mm; the Ausf. D was essentially similar.

In 1940, Sweden ordered 90 tanks but, in July 1940, they were diverted to the Panzer divisions under the designation PzKpfw 38(t) Ausf. S. The PzKpfw 38(t) Ausf. E produced from November 1940 to May 1941 had improved armor. The turret front was thickened by adding a 25mm face-hardened plate over the existing 25mm plate, providing a total of 50mm of protection. Turret side armor was increased to 30mm and the upper front hull was changed to a simple flat plate. The next series of PzKpfw 38(t) Ausf. F was essentially similar to the Ausf. E with very minor production differences and remained in production until October 1941. The PzKpfw 38(t) Ausf. G introduced homogenous 50mm armor instead of the 25+25mm plate used on the previous up-armored types. It was manufactured through June 1942.

Besides the PzKpfw 38(t), the Wehrmacht still used the elderly PzKpfw 35(t). This had a very similar layout to the PzKpfw 38(t) but had an archaic spring suspension. The main problem was its age and approaching mechanical exhaustion. They were sarcastically dubbed "the Škoda Super Sport" by their crew. It was used by only a single unit, Pz.Rgt.11 of the 6.Panzer-Division and all of their tanks were broken down by December 1941.

The Wehrmacht had hoped to use the Czech example to raise two more Panzer divisions from war-booty French tanks. However, the French tanks had poor durability and the two Panzer brigades raised in 1940–41 were relegated to training duty in occupied France.

PzKpfw II

The PzKpfw II remained in widespread service in 1941 even though its combat effectiveness was low due to weak armor and firepower. The Wehrmacht was still short of tanks, and the PzKpfw II was viable for some roles such as scouting and screening missions. It was armed with a 2cm autocannon that was capable of defeating the armor on most older Soviet tanks. The PzKpfw II Ausf. C had been manufactured up to April 1940. It had been up-armored based on experiences in the 1939 Polish campaign where it was vulnerable even to anti-tank rifles. Production of the improved PzKpfw II Ausf. F was delayed until March 1941. This version introduced a simplified frontal armor layout.

A column from Pz.Rgt.25, 7.Panzer-Division led by a PzKpfw II Ausf. C in Lithuania in June 1941.

PzKpfw I

Although the Wehrmacht still had nearly a thousand PzKpfw I in service, very few were deployed in combat due to their age and obsolescence. During the opening phase of the *Barbarossa* campaign, the commander of 17.Panzer-Division, Gen Wilhelm Ritter von Thoma, complained that the PzKpfw I was "a liability for the troops and should be relegated to home defense, coast defense, and training purposes." There is some confusion over the actual number deployed during Operation *Barbarossa* because different quartermaster documents give totals that vary from 96 to 392. The lower figure appears to refer to the basic tank version while the higher figure seems to include the *Kleiner Panzerbefehlswagen* (small command tank) and the *PzKpfw I mit Abwurfvorrichtung*. The command version remained a useful vehicle since its poor armor and firepower was irrelevant to its mission. It was mainly used in battalion and regimental headquarters, signals battalions, and the artillery battalions of the Panzer divisions. The *Abwurfvorrichtung* version was a PzKpfw I Ausf. B fitted with a frame over the rear to deliver high-explosive charges to demolish enemy bunkers.

The PzKpfw I was used in declining numbers during *Barbarossa*. Here, German infantry shelter behind a PzKpfw I Ausf. B of Pz.Abt. z.b.V.40 during fighting near Louhi, south of Lake Tishkeozero near the Murmansk highway. (SA-kuva)

One of the more obscure assault guns was the 15cm sIG33(Sf) auf PzKpfw I Ausf. B which was the standard 15cm heavy infantry gun mounted precariously on a PzKpfw I chassis. This one served in Schwere Infanteriegeschütz (Motorisiert) Kompanie.702 with the 1.Panzer-Division.

Panzerjäger

Following the Battle of France, the HWA continued to convert light tanks into tank destroyers using the 4.7cm gun. The first of these was the 4.7cm PaK(t) auf PzKpfw I Ausf. B that began entering service in April 1940 in time to serve in the 1940 campaign. A total of 202 were converted by February 1941. These were used to form eight Panzerjäger Abteilungen. Six of these battalions as well as two separate companies took part in Operation *Barbarossa* with 150 4.7cm PaK(t) PzKpfw I Ausf. B.

The next light tank destroyer was the 4.7cm PaK(t) auf PzKpfw 35R(f) based on the French Renault R35 infantry tank. Construction began in April 1941 and was completed in October 1941 with a total of 200 conversions. Of the 93 available in June 1941, 81 were deployed with three Panzerjäger Abteilungen for Operation *Barbarossa*. These only lasted until early July as the chassis did not prove to be durable enough for sustained operations and they were withdrawn back to France for training.

The most powerful conversion was the 10.5cm K18 auf Panzer Selbstfahrlafette Iva, nicknamed the Dicker Max. This was not actually a tank destroyer but was intended instead as a bunker-buster to deal with the Stalin line fortifications. This consisted of a 10.5cm K18 field gun mounted on a modified PzKpfw IV chassis in a rear casemate. Only two of these were built, and they served with Panzerjäger-Abteilung.521 in XXIV.Panzer-Korps. One was lost during the fighting near Borisov in the summer of 1941 and the second in 1943.

Sturmgeschütz

"*Gepanzerter Selbstfahrlafette für Sturmgeschütz 7.5cm Kanone Ausf. B*" was the formal name for the vehicle more commonly called the StuG Ausf. B. As its formal name implies, it was an armored, self-propelled vehicle for the 7.5cm assault gun. This gun was an armored counterpart of the infantry's 7.5cm leIG 18 light infantry gun.

D **StuG AUSF. B DURING OPERATION *BARBAROSSA***

1. StuG Ausf. B, StuG.Abt.197, XXXXVIII.Armee Korps (mot.) The StuG battalions typically had a heraldic emblem as their tactical insignia, in this case an Imperial eagle over crossed cannon barrels carried on the front and rear of the vehicle. In some cases, such as this battalion, the *Zug* (platoon) was lettered, in this case "E." The "E" on the hull front in this battalion used a decorative Gothic font but when repeated on the superstructure side, it was in a simpler modern style. German vehicles were often issued with swastika flags in 1941 for aerial recognition.

2. StuG Ausf. B, StuG.Abt.226, IX.Armee Korps (mot.) In the case of this battalion, the unit insignia was a more modern design, a stylized assault gun stenciled in white on the front, sides, and rear. The tactical number of the vehicle was in small white numbers, in this case indicating 2.Batterie, 2.Zug, 1.Geschütze. This unit also used the usual style of German military map symbol in red on the hull side with the battery/battalion number within the tracked symbol.

1

2

The crew of a PzKpfw II Ausf. C of Pz.Abt. z.b.V.40 fit the 2cm KwK30 cannon barrel back into the receiver after cleaning during operations in July 1940.

The StuG Ausf. B had been controversial since its inception because Panzer advocates such as Heinz Guderian had complained that it diverted valuable PzKpfw III chassis away from the Panzer divisions. However, since German infantry divisions lacked any form of tank support, the infantry had pressed for an assault gun as an alternative for the missing infantry tanks. The chassis was essentially the same as that of the PzKpfw III tank, but with a fixed superstructure for the 7.5cm gun. Its role was to provide direct high-explosive firepower to German infantry formations against fortifications and strongpoints. The improved StuG Ausf. D entered production in May 1941 and some were shipped to the Ostfront after the start of Operation *Barbarossa* as replacements.

The basic assault gun formation was the Heeres Sturmgeschütz Abteilung consisting of three batteries. Since these battalions were still relatively new, there were a number of independent batteries in service in 1941. The Sturmgeschütz units were raised and trained by the artillery branch rather than the Panzer force. Although the assault gun force was quite modest in 1941, its proven combat effectiveness led to a constant increase in its size through the war, eventually becoming the most common armored combat vehicle on the Eastern Front by 1944.

The heavy counterpart of the StuG Ausf. B was the 15cm sIG auf PzKpfw I Ausf. B. A total of 38 had been converted in February 1940 by mounting a complete 15cm heavy infantry gun, including its wheels, in a large armored casemate on the front of the hull. The resulting vehicle was very clumsy and no further production was undertaken. Unlike the StuG Ausf. B, they were intended to provide direct fire support in Panzer rather than infantry units. Six companies were deployed in six Panzer divisions in 1940, and again in 1941. These vehicles were mechanically exhausted and survivors were mostly written off by February 1942.

THE CAMPAIGN

Compared to the 1940 campaign, Operation *Barbarossa* was conducted on a much larger battlefield. The German operational goal was to surround and destroy the forward-deployed Red Army units that had moved into occupied eastern Poland and the Baltic countries in 1939–40. Following the initial border battles, the OKH expected that a pause would be necessary at a depth of 300km for the Panzer units to refresh and the trailing infantry divisions to catch up. The OKH anticipated that a second echelon of Red Army formations would

A 4.7cm PaK(t) auf PzKpfw I Ausf. B of Panzerjäger-Abteilung.529, knocked out in the village of Voyny during the fighting near Bryansk in September 1941. The large size of the penetration on the front armor plate suggests it was hit by a high-explosive round.

be located behind the Stalin fortified line behind the pre-1939 Soviet border. The next phase of the campaign would be the encirclement and destruction of this reserve element of the Red Army.

In general, the Wehrmacht expected the Red Army to be formidable in numbers but clumsy in combat. The Germans had witnessed the Red Army first-hand in Poland in 1939 and gained the impression that it was poorly led and poorly trained. The embarrassing performance of the Red Army in Finland in 1939–40 seemed to confirm that the Soviets were incompetent. German planning expected a short campaign concluding the fall of 1941. The strategic goal was to occupy the European portion of the Soviet Union up to a line stretching from Archangel in the Arctic to Astrakhan on the Caspian Sea by the end of 1941.

German preparations for *Barbarossa* were undermined by poor intelligence about the Red Army. The *Fremde Heeres Ost* (FHO: Foreign Armies East) intelligence agency estimated Soviet tank strength as ten armored divisions and 42 moto-mechanized brigades. There were in fact more than 60 Soviet tank divisions. Heinz Guderian's 1937 book *Achtung, Panzer!* had estimated the Red Army tank force at 10,000 tanks. This was widely ridiculed in Berlin even though in fact it underestimated Soviet tank strength by more than half. Hitler later remarked to Guderian that "If I had known that the figures for Russian tank strength that you gave in your book were true, I would not have started this war." It is worth noting that German intelligence also failed to recognize the areas of concentration of the Red Army, especially in Ukraine.

The deployment of the Wehrmacht for *Barbarossa* was channeled by geography. From a mobility perspective, the most significant obstacle was the Pripyat marshland centered on the boundaries of contemporary Belarus and Ukraine. This was unsuitable for mechanized operations and so bifurcated

A PzKpfw IV Ausf. E of Pz.Rgt.33, leads a tank column of 9.Panzer-Division.

the *Barbarossa* battlefield. Three of the four Panzergruppen were assigned routes north of the Pripyat, Panzergruppe.4 heading toward Leningrad through the Baltic states, and Panzergruppen.3 and .2 heading through the Suwałki gap along the Grodno–Minsk–Smolensk "land-bridge" toward Moscow. South of the Pripyat, Panzergruppe.1 was directed into Ukraine.

The one feature underappreciated by the Wehrmacht was the state of Soviet roads. Although Panzer divisions often moved cross-country, for most of the travel, roads were preferred. Roads lowered fuel consumption and reduced the probability of mishaps such as slipping into irrigation ditches or other terrain obstructions. However, the Soviet road network was much poorer than in western Poland or elsewhere in central Europe. There were some highways such as the Minsk–Moscow road, and roads in the vicinity of major Soviet cities were paved and had good bridging. The better roads were assigned to the Panzerkeil as "*Panzerstrasse.*" However, most roads in the rural Soviet Union were not paved. While adequate for local traffic, they soon became rutted from repeated travel by heavy military vehicles. On the dry days of summer, they radiated clouds of choking dust; on wet days, they became gutters of adhesive mud. The Soviet road network would soon reveal itself as an unpredictable adversary to the speedy advance of the Panzerkeil.

Barbarossa unleashed

The start of Operation *Barbarossa* in the pre-dawn hours of June 22, 1941 caught the Red Army largely unprepared. Although many border units suspected that something was amiss in the days prior to the attack, Moscow forbade any actions that might be deemed provocative. The initial Soviet defenses were a belt of rifle divisions and border guard companies stretched linearly along the frontier. Since moving into eastern Poland in September 1939, the Red Army had begun to create the new Molotov defense line of concrete strong points. However, most were incomplete and too few in number when the Germans struck.

The Panzer attacks proceeded as planned on the first days of the invasion, penetrating deep behind the frontier. Some Soviet units defended aggressively, and there were some notable confrontations such as the defense of the old Brest fortress. Most Soviet units were overrun and there were soon thousands of Soviet prisoners of war marching to the rear. Contact with Soviet tanks was very sporadic. The greatest impression was made by the new KV heavy tanks with German units reporting encounters with "80-tonne" monsters. After a week of combat, 1,300 Soviet tanks had been captured or destroyed.

The German intelligence assessment changed alarmingly after the start of the campaign. On July 2, the FHO reported Soviet tank strength to be 15,000 tanks organized into 35

A PzKpfw 38(t) Ausf. G of Pz.Rgt.25, 7.Panzer-Division near Kalvarija, Lithuania, at the start of Operation *Barbarossa*.

A Panzerbefehlswagen Ausf. H of Pz.Rgt.18, 18.Panzer-Division crossing the Bug River near Patulin at the start of Operation *Barbarossa* on June 22, 1941. Four of these command tanks as well as nearly 200 regular gun tanks had been refitted with the *Tauchpanzer* deep wading system, originally developed in 1940 for the aborted Operation *Sea Lion* amphibious invasion of Britain.

armored divisions. Of these, 22 had been located and identified including five in the Far East.

Major tank battles began to erupt in the first week of the campaign as the Soviet mechanized corps close to the frontier began staging counterattacks. In the Heeresgruppe Nord sector, Panzergruppe.4 headed northeast from East Prussia along the main road toward Riga. In the vicinity of Šiauliai in Lithuania, on June 23 the 1. and 6.Panzer-Divisions were struck by the Soviet 28th Tank Division while at the same time, the 2nd Tank Division advanced from the east along the Kaunus road. The Soviet tank units were repulsed after losing more than 60 percent of their tanks, but the fighting became legendary when a single Soviet KV tank of the 4th Regiment, 2nd Tank Division managed to block a crossroads near Raseiniai on June 24–25 in spite of repeated attacks by tanks and anti-tank guns of the 6.Panzer-Division. Another major tank confrontation followed on June 28 when Panzergruppe.4 reached Daugavpils on the Latvian border along the Leningrad road. The 8.Panzer-Division and other German units fought for several days against the Soviet 21st Mechanized Corps, culminating in a battle in the Rēzekne river valley on July 3. In spite of the growing Soviet resistance, Heeresgruppe Nord crossed the Dvina River in multiple locations in the first week of July. The fighting in the Baltic sector from June 22 to July 9 cost the Red Army 2,523 tanks.

On the northern flank of Heeresgruppe Mitte, Panzergruppe.3 first encountered the T-34 tanks of the 5th Tank Division in the battle for the Alytus bridges over the Neman River in Lithuania starting on June 22 while heading for the Lithuanian capital of Vilnius. Although these bridges

E **TANK BATTLE AT DUBNO**

The largest tank battle in history broke out in western Ukraine as Panzergruppe.1 clashed with several Soviet mechanized corps on the first days of Operation *Barbarossa*. This illustration shows PzKpfw III tanks of 16.Panzer-Division during the fighting with the 34th Tank Division of the Soviet 8th Mechanized Corps on June 26–27.

A column of PzKpfw 35(t) tanks of Pz.Rgt.11, 6.Panzer-Division in Lithuania in June 1941. This was the only Panzer division to use the PzKpfw 35(t) during Operation *Barbarossa*.

A pair of PzKpfw III Ausf. J of Pz.Rgt.25 pass the wreck of a PzKpfw 38(t) that has had its turret blown off during the fighting on the Lithuanian border with the Soviet 5th Tank Division on June 22, 1941.

were quickly taken, Heeresgruppe Mitte faced a heavy concentration of over 2,100 Soviet tanks near the critical route along the Minsk–Moscow highway. There were five Soviet mechanized corps in this sector. Hoth's Panzergruppe.3 and Guderian's Panzergruppe.2 enveloped the Soviet forces in the vicinity of the Belarussian capital of Minsk on June 26 and over the next few days trapped and overran several large pockets of Soviet troops in the vicinity. On July 9, Heeresgruppe Mitte reported that it had captured or destroyed 2,585 Soviet tanks in the Białystok/Minsk battles.

The Red Army attempted to halt the German advance along the Minsk–Moscow axis by a counteroffensive between Vitebsk and Orsha starting on July 6. This attack was a failure and led to further encirclements. By July 25, Heeresgruppe Mitte claimed a further 2,030 Soviet tanks in the fighting after Minsk. The Red Army acknowledged losing 4,799 tanks in the defense of the Belarussian sector through July 9. These enormous encirclement victories were dubbed the *Kesselschlachten*, the "Kettle Battles."

These tremendous successes had come at a cost for the Panzer divisions. On July 4, Hoth's Panzergruppe.3 reported that operational tank strength had been reduced to about 50 percent largely because of the poor roads. Dust clogged the air filters, grit clogged tank engines, and there was neither enough fresh oil nor spare engine parts to repair all the dead-lined tanks. The 7.Panzer-Division was fairly typical of Hoth's divisions. They reported that temporary and total losses in the first week of the campaign were 50 percent for the PzKpfw II and PzKpfw III and 75 percent for the PzKpfw IV. Some of the temporary losses were repaired and put back into service. But on July 21, the 7.Panzer-Division reported only 29 percent of its tanks operational while 77 of its original 276 tanks (28 percent) were total losses.

On July 7, Guderian's neighboring Panzergruppe.2 reported to Berlin that the 3. and 18.Panzer-Division had operational tank rates of 35 percent, 4. and 17.Panzer-Division reported 60 percent and 10.Panzer-Division reported 80 percent. By July 17, 4.Panzer-Division had been reduced to only 40 serviceable tanks, 24 percent of its starting strength. The 10.Panzer-Division was down to 30 percent of its tanks still serviceable.

On July 5, Panzergruppe.1 in Ukraine reported that "After 14 days of combat we have an estimated 100 Panzers totally lost… From experience there will be at least the same or double the number temporarily out of action. This means that about 55 percent are still operational."

The low operational rate was in part due to an underestimation of the amount of spare parts needed. The quartermaster of Panzergruppe.1 on July 3 reported that "the many Panzers that are in the workshops due to a shortage of parts and cannot be returned to service is extremely regrettable and greatly reduces the number of combat-ready tanks. Under these circumstances roughly 50 percent of the Panzers cannot be repaired." About 70 percent of the Panzers

A PzKpfw IV Ausf. D, tactical number 622 of II./Pz.Rgt.25, 7.Panzer-Division drives through the Lithuanian capital of Vilnius in early July following its capture on June 24.

that were dead-lined in divisional workshops needed spare parts to return to service.

The tank fighting between Heeresgruppe Süd and the Red Army's forward-deployed Kiev Military District in Galicia were the largest tank battles in history. There were seven Soviet mechanized corps in the area totaling over 4,300 tanks of which more than 760 were modern types such as the T-34 and KV. Facing them were the five Panzer divisions of Kleist's Panzergruppe.1 totaling about 780 tanks. The Soviet 4th and 8th Mechanized Corps stationed near Lvov attempted to counterattack the invading German forces near Nemirov and Radzekhov on June 22–23, but were repulsed. The 11.Panzer-Division spearheaded a breakthrough toward Dubno on June 24–25, creating a deep bulge into Soviet lines. The Soviets counterattacked with the 8th and 15th Mechanized Corps from the south near Brody and with the 9th and 19th Mechanized Corps from the north near Rovno. Intense tank fighting continued through the end of June as the Red Army rushed reinforcements into the sector. By July 1, 11.Panzer-Division had raced ahead to Shepetivka, a rail junction on the Goryn River while the 13.Panzer-Division and 14.Panzer-Division reached the old fortress city

A column of PzKpfw 38(t) of Pz.Rgt.25, 7.Panzer-Division at dawn on June 22, 1941 on the Prussia/Lithuanian frontier at the start of Operation *Barbarossa*. The lead tank is a PzKpfw 38(t) E/F in the *Befehlswagen* configuration for platoon commanders with the hull machine gun deleted to permit the use of an Fu 5 radio transceiver.

of Novgorod-Volynskiy. The German forces eventually overwhelmed the Red Army units still in the Galician pocket.

Panzergruppe.1 suffered 85 total tank losses up to July 5 and 117 up to July 11. Operational tank strength had been reduced from 780 to 430 tanks on June 5 with about 200 tanks under repair due to battle damage and breakdowns. Soviet tank losses in the Galicia–Volyn sector through July 6 were 4,381 tanks due to enormous numbers of abandoned and broken-down tanks.

After the first two weeks of fighting along the frontier, the Wehrmacht had

A PzKpfw IV Ausf. E, tactical number 1201 of III./ Pz.Rgt.25, one of four knocked out on June 22, 1941 during fighting with the Soviet 5th Tank Division near Alytus during the fighting for the Neman river bridges.

successfully broken through in all sectors and enveloped and destroyed a significant fraction of Red Army forces. Soviet tank losses through July 9 had been over 11,700 tanks, about half of pre-war strength, but most of the forward-deployed tank force. Berlin was optimistic that *Barbarossa*'s goals were within reach. German tanks losses had been significant, with about 700 total losses and a similar number in repair due to battle damage and mechanical problems. The Panzer divisions still had about 50–60 percent of their tanks operational.

There were no plans to dispatch new replacement tanks to the Ostfront in spite of the losses. At a meeting at the OKH headquarters on July 8, Hitler explained why he wanted new production tanks to be reserved in Germany rather than being sent to the Ostfront as replacements: "He wants to make sure that we will have brand-new weapons for the missions still ahead... The tank losses suffered since the beginning of the campaign therefore necessitate a reduction in the number of Panzer divisions [on the Ostfront]. The personnel freed up will serve as the crews for the new tanks in Germany." Four new Panzer divisions were organized in 1941 and three more in early 1942, numbered 21.Panzer-Division to 27.Panzer-Division.

Nevertheless, on July 8, Hitler relented and authorized the shipment of 35 PzKpfw 38(t), 50 PzKpfw III, and 15 PzKpfw IV to the Ostfront, equivalent to less than 15 percent of the total losses suffered to date. On August 16, the OKH formally requested the transfer of a further 180 tanks from the reserves in Germany consisting of 40 PzKpfw 38(t), 100 PzKpfw III and 40 PzKpfw IV. This request was denied by Hitler.

Hitler was so optimistic about the prospects for victory that he was already planning for a renewed campaign against Britain once Moscow had been subdued. He envisioned the need to create or transfer at least ten Panzer divisions after the conclusion of *Barbarossa* for contingencies in Norway, Portugal/Spain, and the mid-East. On July 14, Hitler decreed that priority would shift away from the army in favor of the Luftwaffe and Kriegsmarine for the renewed campaign against Britain. As a result, the number of planned infantry divisions was reduced, and correspondingly, production of the StuG Ausf. B assault gun was trimmed from 50 to 25 per month. The summer cutbacks had lingering effects and production of weapons for the army fell by 29 percent between July and December 1941.

Blitzkrieg bogs down

As the Panzerkeil continued to push deeper into the Soviet Union, attrition increased due to the poor roads and more frequent mechanical breakdowns. GenMaj Walther Nehring, commander of the 18.Panzer-Division, remarked that "This situation and its consequences will become unsustainable in the future if we do not want to be destroyed by winning." At a meeting at Hitler's headquarters on July 13, Gen Walther Buhle, chief of the organizations section of the OKH, reported that average Panzer division operational strength had fallen to about 50 percent from the start of the campaign.

The crew of a Panzerbefehlswagen Ausf. H tries to extricate their command tank after it has come to grief in an irrigation ditch alongside a road south of Kalvarija, Lithuania, on the first day of Operation *Barbarossa*. The tactical number III01 indicates the battalion executive officer of Stabskompanie, III.Abteilung, Pz.Rgt.25.

Heeresgruppe Mitte reached Smolensk on the main Moscow road on July 16, but the Panzer spearheads were increasingly running out of momentum. The 19.Panzer-Division captured Velikie Luki on July 19, but was abruptly kicked out by a vigorous Soviet counterattack. Unlike the early encirclement battles near the frontier, the destruction of the massive pocket east of Smolensk would take weeks of fighting. The status of the Panzerkeil continued to deteriorate due to steady attrition. On July 29, Guderian's Panzergruppe.2 reported that only 286 tanks were operational, 29 percent of its original strength. Worse still, of these 238 operational tanks, 128 were PzKpfw II and four were PzKpfw I light tanks. There were only 97 PzKpfw III and 38 PzKpfw IV spread through Panzergruppe.2's five Panzer divisions, only 20 percent of its original medium tank strength. The collapsing number of operational tanks could also be seen in the decline in fuel and ammunition consumption by Panzergruppe.2. Fuel consumption fell more than half from 30,280 tonnes in July to only 14,730 in August and likewise ammunition consumption fell from 22,100 tonnes to only 10,465 tonnes in August.

Historian David Stahel has dubbed the battle of the Smolensk pocket "the end of Blitzkrieg" since it revealed the inability of the Wehrmacht to conduct mobile operations for much more than a month due to mechanical exhaustion, combat attrition, and overstretched logistics. This might have been anticipated by the lessons of the French campaign but it was not. The Smolensk pocket was not finally sealed until August 5. By this stage, most of the forward-deployed Soviet mechanized corps had been destroyed in the previous border battles. A total of 1,348 Soviet tanks were lost in the defense of the Smolensk pocket. The performance of Heeresgruppe Mitte with its heavy concentration of Panzers was essential to the success of *Barbarossa*. By the end of July, its momentum had been exhausted.

In early August, the Panzer divisions of the Heeresgruppe Mitte's two Panzer groups were pulled out of the line for refitting. There were very few replacement tanks and even spare parts were at a premium. The first major tank repair depot on the Ostfront had been established at Orsha in Belarus. By July 29, it had received 110 new engines for the PzKpfw 38(t) and PzKpfw

German infantry under the cover of a pair of PzKpfw 35(t) of I./Pz.Rgt.11, 6.Panzer-Division advance through a village during the operations of Panzergruppe.4 in the Baltics in the summer of 1941.

III of the 250 requested. Responding to growing complaints by the field commanders for more tanks and spares, at an OKH meeting on August 4, Hitler defended his parsimony in replacement tanks for the Ostfront, offering instead to ship 350 replacement engines. In fact, this had already been authorized by the OKH but Hitler's approval led to a speedier delivery of the engines by air transport.

When the refitting program was completed on August 21, the operational strength was about 900 tanks or 43.5 percent of starting strength. Hoth's Panzergruppe.3 had slightly over 400 tanks and Guderian's Panzergruppe.2 about 495.

The XXIV.Panzer Korps in Guderian's Panzergruppe.2 warned that the repairs on many tanks were only temporary: "Every Panzer is only provisionally fit for service. As a result of oil shortages, no oil changes could be undertaken. If the Panzers are committed to a large-scale operation in their current condition, then their total loss must be expected." The corps' 4.Panzer-Division was a good example of the fragility of the mechanically exhausted Panzer force. On August 20 it reported that it had been reduced to

F

FLAMMPANZER DURING OPERATION *BARBAROSSA*

1. PzKpfw II (F) Ausf. A, 3.Kompanie, Panzer-Abteilung (Flamm).101. The PzKpfw II (F) were finished in the usual overall RAL 7021 Dunkelgrau. This example from 3.Kompanie has the usual style of three-digit tactical number. This unit originally used an insignia of crossed flamethrowers in light green. In 1941, this insignia was changed to a multi-color flame as seen here. The exact colors are unrecorded but presumably orange and white. Its sister unit, the Panzer-Abteilung (Flamm).100 used a yellow *Wolfsangel* (Wolf trap) painted on the hull side as seen here in the inset illustration.

2. PzKpfw B2 (F), 2.Kompanie, Panzer-Abteilung (Flamm).102. The HWA intended to convert most of its war-booty French Char B1 bis into a flamethrower tank using a Daimler-Benz system. When this was not ready in time for Operation *Barbarossa*, HWA selected a *Zwischenlösung* (interim design). Two different interim types were used, in this case, the same turreted Wegmann flamethrower used with the PzKpfw II (F). The flame turret was mounted on a shelf on the hull gun mantlet, with the flame fuel and compressed air tanks placed inside. This battalion used a *Feuerdrache (*Firedrake) insignia, painted on the rear of the hull side. Each company had 12 flamethrower tanks in three platoons (*Zug*) so the tactical number on this tank indicates 2. Kompanie, 2.Zug, Panzer.4.

1

2

A PzKpfw II (F) Flamingo tank carefully negotiates a German engineer bridge over the Dnepr River in July 1941 during the advance on Smolensk. Two battalions of these flamethrower tanks participated in *Barbarossa*. This particular example was from the first batch of conversions based on the PzKpfw II Ausf. D.

44 serviceable tanks, only 26 percent of its starting strength. Two days later its strength increased to 64 tanks due to the hasty repair effort. A week later on August 29, 4.Panzer-Division's operational strength had collapsed to 15 tanks since these were the only ones with sufficient oil.

The situation was similar on the other fronts. On July 20, Panzergruppe.1 with Heeresgruppe Süd in Ukraine reported that the operational strength of its Panzer divisions had fallen to about 40 percent with 16.Panzer-Division slightly worse and 13.Panzer-Division and 14.Panzer-Division somewhat better. The plan was to call a ten-day halt after reaching the Dnepr River to give the Panzer units time to repair and rebuild their tanks. It was hoped that this halt would allow the readiness rate on tanks to come up to about 60–70 percent. On July 23, Buhle reported that only about 20 percent of Panzer casualties were total losses but that crew casualties were high and officer losses in some divisions were as great as 50 percent. Buhle noted that since Heeresgruppe Süd had crossed the Berezina River, dust ingestion and subsequent engine damage had been the main source of tank casualties. The temporary halt resulted in an increase in the tank readiness rate in Heeresgruppe Süd to about 60 percent by August 19, though it was acknowledged that the status of many tanks remained marginal.

Operational tank strength in Panzergruppe.1, June–August 1941									
Unit	Jun 22	Jun 30	Jul 5	Jul 11	Jul 18	Jul 30	Aug 5	Aug 11	Aug 18
9.Pz.Div.	131	86	67	56	66	64	63	92	79
11.Pz.Div.	144	103	87	91	82	81	69	64	75
13.Pz.Div.	146	110	96	97	94	96	101	95	61
14.Pz.Div.	146	110	91	115	95	90	90	104	104
16.Pz.Div.	145	109	90	21	35	59	56	66	61
Total	712	518	431	380	372	390	379	421	380
Percent	*100*	*72.7*	*60.5*	*53.4*	*52.2*	*54.8*	*53.2*	*59.1*	*53.4*

On July 22, 1941, the loader of a PzKpfw IV Ausf. E of Pz.Rgt.6, 3.Panzer-Division leans out of the turret to keep an eye on the edge of the temporary plank roadway added by German engineers over a Soviet railway bridge to permit tanks to pass.

On August 28, OKH reported to Hitler on the status of the Panzer divisions on the Ostfront. Total losses of armored vehicles by the end of August were 1,488; only 96 replacement tanks had arrived. At the start of September 1941, the Panzer divisions on average had 47 percent of their tanks operational, 23 percent under repair and 30 percent lost. Compared to a similar report on August 4, the percentage of total losses had increased from 20 to 30 percent in a month's time while the percentage of tanks in repair had fallen from 30 to 23 percent. The conditions of the Panzer units differed from sector to sector as is shown on this quartermaster report from September 4, 1941. The two Panzergruppen of Heeresgruppe Mitte that had borne the brunt of the fighting suffered markedly higher losses than the other two army groups.

Panzergruppe status, (%) September 4, 1941

Status	Panzergruppe.4	Panzergruppe.3	Panzergruppe.2	Panzergruppe.1
Operational	69.3	40.8	25.4	53.0
In repair	12.0	25.0	42.3	23.5
Total loss	18.7	34.0	32.7	23.5

The actual strength of tanks in the Panzer divisions varied from day to day. As the summer dragged on, the availability of spare parts within the divisional maintenance echelon deteriorated badly and many units cannibalized other tanks for parts. Many repaired tanks were only marginally functional with lingering mechanical issues. One report indicated that about a third of the repaired tanks would break down again within 50km once the fighting resumed.

Panzer status on Ostfront, early September 1941

Status	Pz.I	Pz.II	Pz.35(t)	Pz.38(t)	Pz.III	Pz.IV	Bef.Pz.III	Percent
Operational	108	458	102	249	404	193	159	45.9
In repair	41	146	8	194	387	133	27	25.7
Replacements			2	42	35	9		2.4
Losses	172	152	47	184	232	125	38	26.0

A Panzerbefehlswagen Ausf. H command tank of Pz.Rgt.36, 14.Panzer-Division camouflaged in a corn field outside Krivoi Rog during the fighting by Heeresgruppe Süd in Ukraine on August 4, 1941.

On to Kiev

While the main thrust toward Moscow was stalled along the highway east of Smolensk, Heeresgruppe Süd had been stymied by the enormous concentration of Soviet forces in Ukraine. The original Wehrmacht intelligence assessments had not recognized that the Red Army had considered Ukraine to be the operational focus of its defense and had positioned its forces accordingly. One option was to detach elements of Heeresgruppe Mitte to strike southward to facilitate the capture of Kiev. By late August, Heeresgruppe Mitte was deep enough east that it was past the terrain obstacle posed by the Pripyat marshlands that had previously separated it from Heeresgruppe Süd. In a controversial decision, the drive to Moscow was held in abeyance until Kiev and the Red Army forces in Ukraine were overwhelmed. The formal order for the attack on Kiev was issued by the OKH on August 30, temporarily shifting the focal point of *Barbarossa* from Heeresgruppe Mitte to Heeresgruppe Süd.

A StuG Ausf. B of StuG-Abt. 243 in the summer of 1941. This assault gun battalion saw its combat debut on the Ostfront in August 1941, supporting the 1.Gebirgs-Division in Ukraine with Heeresgruppe Süd.

Guderian's Panzergruppe.2 had already been directed to begin moving south several days earlier. Their 3.Panzer-Division seized the Desna river bridge at Novhorod-Severskiy on August 26, marking the start of their southward offensive. By mid-September, the German pincer movement from north and south had trapped an enormous Soviet force in a pocket stretching from Kiev eastward. On September 17, Stalin belatedly authorized the Red Army to withdraw from Kiev. Fighting for the Kiev pocket lasted through September 24 with nearly 435,000 Soviet troops caught in the encirclement. It was noteworthy that Soviet tank losses in the Kiev defensive operation were only 411 tanks, a testament to the enormous scale of destruction in the earlier border battles in June and July and the Red Army's resultant weakness in tanks.

A pair of PzKpfw II Ausf. C of Pz.Rgt.15, 11.Panzer-Division cross the Dnepr River in Ukraine in September 1941 on an engineer pontoon ferry during the Kiev campaign by Heeresgruppe Süd.

The succession of encirclement battles fought in the western Soviet Union in June–September 1941 left large groups of Soviet troops in isolated pockets in the countryside. While most of these were mopped up by subsequent waves of German infantry divisions, some coalesced to form partisan groups that staged raids in the German rear areas. In response to this threat, on July 23 the OKH decided to establish special security tank platoons in rear area divisions, with regular infantry divisions to be authorized six platoons with 4–5 tanks each while security divisions were authorized a single tank platoon. These platoons were to be created using Beutepanzer (war-booty tanks). The first 40 French Renault FT and R35 tanks were delivered to security companies in September 1941, but mainly to deal with the partisan threat in Yugoslavia. A further 45 Renault R35 were shipped in mid-September. By November 1941, there were about 110 French Beutepanzer in use in rear areas of the Ostfront, with additional Soviet tanks pressed into use by various German infantry and police units. The OKH planned to have about 550 French Beutepanzer available on the Ostfront by February–March 1942 with about 380 more on the Süd-Ostfront in Yugoslavia.

Operation *Taifun*

By the conclusion of the Kiev campaign, Hitler and OKH realized that the *Barbarossa* plan had been derailed and its objectives were unlikely to be met in 1941. The focus shifted back to the capture of Moscow, with a new plan codenamed Operation *Taifun* (Typhoon). This obviously required a reinvigoration of the two Panzer groups of Heeresgruppe Mitte. On September 15, Hitler finally agreed to authorize Panzer replacements in time for the start of *Taifun*. This included 60 PzKpfw 38(t), 150 PzKpfw III, and 96 PzKpfw IV, but this was still only a third of the 815 tanks manufactured in June–August 1941.

By late September, Heeresgruppe Mitte's operational tank strength had fallen to about 750 tanks in its original Panzer divisions, or about 30.2 percent of its starting strength. Guderian's Panzergruppe.2 had an operational tank strength of 280 tanks, 31 percent of its starting strength. Hoth's Panzergruppe.3 had significant shortages with 19.Panzer-Division having only 70 operational

A StuG Ausf. B assault gun of StuG.Abt.244 during the fighting for Ivankovo, 30km north of Kiev, in October 1941.

tanks and 20.Panzer-Division having only 44. Replacements were promised that would bring 19.Panzer-Division to a strength of 90 tanks and 20.Panzer-Division to 74 tanks. For Operation *Taifun*, Heeresgruppe Mitte was reinforced by the arrival of two fresh Panzer divisions, the 2.Panzer-Division. and 5.Panzer-Division, adding about 450 new tanks to its strength. In addition, Panzergruppe.4, formerly assigned to the advance on Leningrad, was redirected to assist in *Taifun*.

At the start of Operation *Taifun*, the OKH reported that Panzergruppe.4 was in the best shape with nearly total operational strength in its Panzer units. Guderian's Panzergruppe.2 was rated at 50–60 percent operational tank strength, while Hoth's Panzergruppe.3 and Kleist's Panzergruppe.1 were at about 70–80 percent. Facing them on the Red Army's Western and Bryansk Fronts were only about 720 Soviet tanks of which merely 134 were T-34 tanks.

Operation *Taifun* started on October 2 with exceptionally good weather that assisted the advance of the Panzer divisions. The offensive proceeded toward Moscow from the southwest along the main highway toward Bryansk. The Soviet Western Front attempted to respond, but within days, Heeresgruppe Mitte managed to trap a large pocket of Soviet formations along the road from Yartsevo to Vyazma. The first snow of the year arrived on October 6, a hint of an unusually cold winter about to arrive. According to Heeresgruppe Mitte, the ensuing reduction of the pockets led to the capture of 673,098 Soviet troops and 1,277 tanks. This was the largest encirclement of the 1941 campaign, though the number of captured Soviet tanks was relatively low simply due to weak state of the Soviet tank force at

G AXIS ALLY TANKS DURING OPERATION *BARBAROSSA*

1. Toldi light tank, 2nd Reconnaissance Brigade, Hungarian I.Fast Corps, 1941. In 1941, the *Honvéd* (Hungarian armed forces) adopted "French camouflage" consisting of a base coat of army dark olive green (~FS 34096) with splotches of ochre (~FS 30266) and chocolate brown (~FS 30059). The national insignia was the Balkan cross, but with the cross itself painted in green and the corners of the symbol filled in with red to create the national colors of green/white/red. The 2nd Reconnaissance Brigade had the cross imposed on a red circle rather than the more typical octagon shape. The *Honvéd* crest was applied as a decal on the turret side immediately in front of the turret side hatches. The license plate at the rear consisted of the letter H (*Honvéd*), a shield in the national colors, and a three-digit registration number. Vehicles of the 2nd Reconnaissance Brigade were often marked with "2.F." with the abbreviation for the unit designation in Hungarian (*2.felderítő dandár*).

2. R-2c light tank, Regimentul 1 Care de Luptă , 3rd Romanian Army, Ukraine 1941. The Romanian R-2 tanks were delivered from Škoda in Czechoslovak Kaki, an olive drab color. The production serial number was painted on the hull side in black in the sequence Sr. 1 to Sr. 126. The national insignia was the *Crucea Mihai* (Michael's Cross) carried as a simple white stencil on the forward hull side, and in color like those of the Romanian air force on the engine deck for aerial recognition. The tanks also carried the royal crest on the forward side of the turret, in a very dark shade of olive drab. However, this did not offer good contrast and is barely visible in most photos. The tanks carried a three-digit tactical number, stenciled in white on the rear turret sides, in this case indicating 2nd company, 3rd platoon, 4th tank.

the time due to the massive summer tank losses. The German tank casualties were 50 total losses plus a significant number of damaged tanks. The battles of Bryansk and Vyazma were the zenith of Operation *Taifun*.

One organizational change that took place during Operation *Taifun* was the redesignation of the Panzer groups as Panzer armies. Panzergruppe1. and Panzergruppe.2 became the 1.Panzerarmee and 2.Panzerarmee in early October; Pz.Gp.3 and Pz.Gp.4 were renamed in January–February 1942.

Although the Wehrmacht reached the gates of Moscow, the attack stalled and the Soviet counteroffensive threw the Germans back. This was the end of Operation *Taifun* and the first strategic German defeat in 1941. On December 22, a report on the 16 Panzer divisions of Heeresgruppe Nord and Heeresgruppe Mitte reported on their remaining strength as detailed in the chart here. The operational Panzer strength of two army groups had been reduced to that of two Panzer divisions.

Panzer status of HG Nord and HG Mitte, December 22, 1941

Status	PzKpfw II	PzKpfw 38(t)	PzKpfw III	PzKpfw IV	Total
Operational	66	84	180	75	405
In repair	188	202	254	136	780
Total	*254*	*286*	*434*	*211*	*1,185*

By the end of December 1941, the Wehrmacht had lost 2,839 tanks (66.1 percent) on the Ostfront compared to total Soviet tank losses of 20,500. StuG losses through February 1942 were 159 of which nearly all were on the Ostfront.

Wehrmacht tank losses, June–December 1941*

Type	Jun	Jul	Aug	Sep	Oct	Nov	Dec	Total
PzKpfw I	34	146	171	7	18	33	19	428
PzKpfw II	16	117	106	32	65	30	92	458
PzKpfw 35(t)	11	9	23	5	49	22	3	122
PzKpfw 38(t)	33	182	183	62	85	149	102	796
PzKpfw III (3.7cm)	23	59	25	16	11	13	28	175
PzKpfw III (5cm)	27	164	78	104	79	116	208	776
PzKpfw IV	16	111	70	23	55	38	65	378
PzBefWg	1	18	11	17	10	6	28	91
StuG III	3	11	26	12	23	10	19	104
Total	164	817	693	278	395	417	564	3,328
Ostfront Losses	*118*	*732*	*638*	*257*	*337*	*382*	*375*	*2,839*

*Some types such as the PzKpfw II (F) and Beutepanzer losses not included

BATTLE ANALYSIS

The failure of the Panzerkeil in 1941 doomed Operation *Barbarossa*. This was not due to the failure of German Panzer divisions so much as it was a failure at the strategic level in Berlin. The rapid victories of 1939–40 made Berlin overconfident about the ability to win quick and easy victories. There was a fundamental failure by Hitler and the OKH to appreciate the dimensional and temporal difference between the campaign in France in 1940 and a war

A PzKpfw III Ausf. G advances toward the wreck of a burning Soviet T-28 medium tank during the August 1941 fighting.

in the Soviet Union. The distances involved were substantially different, and the Wehrmacht did not have the logistical capability to conduct sustained, high-tempo maneuver operations to the depths required to seize Moscow. The road distance from the German frontier to Dunkirk was 380km; the distance from occupied Poland to Moscow was three times as great. The campaign in France and Belgium was waged on good roads with ample opportunities to exploit local supplies of fuel and oil. The campaign in the Soviet Union was waged along rutted farm roads alternately enveloped in choking dust or reduced to muddy gulleys by summer and fall rain.

The durability of the Panzers was as good or better than the tanks of their opponents, nevertheless the Panzerkeil became mechanically exhausted after only a few months of combat operations. Berlin expected too much of the existing technology and had not anticipated the need for more replacement tanks and more spare parts as the campaign progressed.

Berlin was lulled into false optimism in June and July 1941 by the stunning tactical victories of the Panzerkeil in the border encirclement battles. The enormous destruction wreaked on the Red Army in June and early July suggested that victory would soon be forthcoming. Hitler and the OKH ignored warnings from the Panzergruppe commanders about the dwindling combat effectiveness of the Panzer divisions in the face of steady combat attrition and mechanical exhaustion the deeper they penetrated into the Soviet Union. By the end of summer, the Panzerkeil was exhausted and soon victory was beyond their grasp.

The German Panzer force completely dominated the Soviet tank force in the first three months of fighting. The initial border battles cost the Red Army some 15,500 tanks; a catastrophe later dubbed "the tank massacre" (*tankoviy pogrom*) by Russian historians. The reasons for this were the experience and training of the German Panzer units, rather than any technological advantage of the Panzers over Soviet tanks. By 1941, the Panzer divisions could rely on a cadre of experienced tank crews and unit commanders hardened by their combat experiences in Poland, France, and

A PzKpfw III Ausf. J of Panzergruppe.3 knocked out in the fighting in the village of Talachyn (Tolotschin) in Belarus on July 14, 1941. The extent of the damage to the front plates suggests it was hit by large-caliber high-explosive artillery projectiles rather than armor-piercing tank gun projectiles.

the Balkans. In contrast, the Soviet tank force was in turmoil due to the political excesses of the Stalinist state, the lack of experienced small-unit commanders, and amateur tank crews. The Soviet predicament is explained in more depth in the accompanying book of this series on tanks of the Red Army in *Barbarossa*.[2]

The majority of Soviet tank casualties were not caused by direct tank-vs-tank duels. Most Soviet tanks were lost due to mechanical breakdowns or accidents on the way to the battlefield, or abandonment during the great encirclement battles of June–July 1941. The enormous disparity in tank losses in 1941, roughly 7-to-1, was also due to the law of mechanized warfare that whoever retains the battlefields reduces their own tank casualties while amplifying enemy losses. The Wehrmacht could recover and repair their damaged tanks; the Red Army could not.

The combat effectiveness of German versus Soviet tanks is difficult to summarize in the short space available here since there were so many different types used by the opposing sides. Except for the new Soviet T-34 and KV tanks, the technical features of the opposing tanks were similar. Armor protection on the newer German tanks such as the late production PzKpfw III and PzKpfw IV was generally better than on the most common Soviet types such as the T-26 and BT-7. However, many German tanks including the PzKpfw II, PzKpfw 38(t), and older PzKpfw III and PzKpfw IV had armor levels similar to the Soviet tanks and were vulnerable to the ubiquitous Soviet 45mm gun.[3] In terms of firepower, the German 3.7cm and Soviet 45mm tank guns were comparable, though the German tanks had an accuracy advantage due to better tank telescopes. In terms of mobility, neither side had any notable advantages.

The areas of distinct German technical advantage were in situational awareness and command and control. Another rule of mechanized warfare is that who sees first and engages first usually wins the tank duel. This requires

2   Soviet Tanks in Barbarossa 1941, Steven Zaloga, Osprey NVG 342, 2025.
3   For a direct comparison between the PzKpfw 38(t) and BT-7, see: Steven Zaloga, *Panzer 38(t) vs BT-7: Barbarossa 1941*, Osprey Duel 78, 2017.

The three-man turret layout of the PzKpfw III and PzKpfw IV was a decided advantage in tank combat. The cupola on the roof gave the tank commander excellent visibility of the surrounding battlefield compared to the constricted viewing devices on Soviet tanks. (SA-kuva)

situational awareness that can be achieved both by crew performance and the technical layout of the tank. The PzKpfw III and PzKpfw IV both had three-man turrets. This permitted the tank commander to focus on leading his tank in battle and not on distractions such as loading the tank gun. In addition, these tanks were fitted with all-around vision cupolas that permitted the tank commander to observe the surrounding terrain from under armored cover. These cupolas were also designed to permit the tank commander to fight with his head outside the turret for a better view. Soviet tanks such as the T-26 and BT-7 had two-man turrets. The commander had secondary tasks such as loading the tank gun. Furthermore, vision devices were limited to archaic periscopes. Soviet turret hatches opened forward, making it difficult for the commander to observe with his head out of the turret.

Finally, the German tanks had more radios, and their radios were better quality. The lack of radios in Soviet tanks and the number of radios in German tanks has been misunderstood and the disparity was not as great as it has often been portrayed. Soviet tanks were commonly fitted with radios, though not as extensively as in German tanks. For example, of the 7,485 T-26 gun tanks in service in 1941, 3,440 (46 percent) had radios. However, the radios were often in poor repair, had fragile antennas, and depended on telegraphic communication at longer ranges in an army chronically short of skilled crews. The German advantage in radios has often been exaggerated with claims that all German tanks had radios. While all German tanks had radio receivers, only platoon commanders had radio transmitter/receivers. In other words, only the platoon commander could actually talk to the other tanks while the remainder of the platoon could only listen. Furthermore, the German AM radios had distinct limitations especially during tank movement since the metal-on-metal contact of track and suspension as well as vibration interfered with radio transmission and reception. Nevertheless, the greater number of German tank radios and their better quality were a significant tactical advantage in maneuver warfare.

The Soviet shortcomings in situational awareness and command and control were exacerbated by the poor level of crew training in 1941. German accounts of tank fighting frequently compared Soviet tank formations to a

A platoon of PzKpfw III Ausf. H tanks of Panzerarmee.1 advance through Rostov-on-Don during the fighting there in November 1941.

hen with her chicks. The junior tanks in a platoon would blindly follow the platoon leader since they lacked the experience and situational awareness to operate independently.

Ultimately, the Wehrmacht's failure in 1941 was due to broader strategic misjudgments rather than specific technical shortcomings of the Panzer force. Generalfeldmarschall Albert Kesselring later concluded that

> The Panzergruppen were too weak. Our strategic mechanized forces had to be proportionate to the breadth and depth of the area to be conquered and the strength of the enemy. We had nowhere near this strength. Our tracked vehicles, including tanks, were not sufficiently durable. There were technical limitations to constant movement. A mobile operation to a depth of 1,000 kilometers through strongly defended enemy territory requires vast supplies, especially if there is no chance of exploiting large and useful enemy material.

FURTHER READING

This short bibliography covers some of the historical surveys of Operation *Barbarossa*. The many monographs on various types of Panzers have been omitted due to space, but Tom Jentz's Panzer Tracts series is always a good start. Nigel Askey's multi-volume series on *Barbarossa* provides a particularly rich source of data on the campaign. The Stahel trilogy is a fresh assessment of Germany's war aims and provides a provocative look at the reasons for the Wehrmacht's failure in 1941. The author also used numerous archival records from Record Group 242 (Captured German Records) at the US National Archives and Records Administration (NARA II) at College Park, Maryland. Unless otherwise noted, the photos here are from NARA II and the author's collection.

Askey, Nigel, *Operation Barbarossa: The Complete Organisational and Statistical Analysis and Military Simulation, Vol. I, IIA, and IIB*, Lulu Publishing, 2013

Boog, Horst et al., *Germany and the Second World War Volume IV: The Attack on the Soviet Union*, Oxford University Press, Oxford, 1998

Crippa, Paolo and Antonio Tallillo, *Italian Armoured Vehicles in Russia 1941–1944*, Soldiershop, Zanica, 2022

De Beaulieu, Charles, *Leningrad: The Advance of Panzer Group 4, 1941*, Casemate, Havertown, 2020

Forczyk, Robert, *Tank Warfare on the Eastern Front 1941–42*, Pen & Sword, Barnsley, 2013

Halder, GenOberst Franz, *War Journal of Franz Halder, Vol. VI, Feb 21, 1941–Jul 31, 1941; Vol. VII, Aug 1, 1941– Sep 24, 1942*, HQ, USA-Europe Historical Division, 1947

Hofmann, Gen d.Inf. Rudolf and GenMaj Alfred Toppe, *Consumption and Attrition Rates in the Operations of German Army Group Center in Russia 1941*, Foreign Military Studies P-190, HQ, USA-Europe Historical Division, 1953

Hoth, Hermann, *Panzer Operations: Panzer Group 3 during the Invasion of Russia 1941*, Casemate, Havertown, 2015

Jentz, Thomas, *Panzer Truppen: The Complete Guide to the Creation & Combat Employment of Germany's Tank Force, Vol. 1: 1933–1942*, Shiffer, Atglen, 1996

Kavalerchik, Boris, *The Tanks of Operation Barbarossa*, Pen & Sword, Barnsley, 2018

Kiliment, Charles and Bretislav Naklada, *Germany's First Ally: Armed Forces of the Slovak State 1939–1945*, Schiffer, Atglen, 1997

Muikku, Esa and Jukka Purhonnen, *Suomalaiset Panssarivaunet 1918–1997*, Apali, Helsinki, 1997

Mujzer, Peter, *Huns on Wheels: Hungarian Mobile Forces in WWII*, Mujzer, Budapest, 2014

Munzel, Oskar, *Panzer Tactics: Tank Operations in the East 1941–42*, Casemate, Havertown, 2021

Scafes, Cornel et al., *Trupele Blindate din Armata Romana 1919–1947*, Muzeul Militar National, Bucharest, 2005

Stahel, David, *Kiev 1941: Hitler's Battle for Supremacy in the East*, Cambridge University Press, Cambridge, 2013

Stahel, David, *Operation Barbarossa and Germany's Defeat in the East*, Cambridge University Press, Cambridge, 2009

Stahel, David, *Operation Typhoon: Hitler's March on Moscow*, Cambridge University Press, Cambridge, 2013

INDEX

Note: Page locators in bold refer to plate captions, pictures and illustrations.All matèriel is German unless otherwise stated.